BRING ME MY MACHINE GUN

*The Battle for the Soul of South Africa
from Mandela to Zuma*

Alec Russell

PUBLICAFFAIRS
New York

Published in the United States by PublicAffairs™, a member of the Perseus Books Group.

PublicAffairs books are available at special discounts for bulk purchases in the U.S. by corporations, institutions, and other organizations. For more information, please contact the Special Markets Department at the Perseus Books Group, 2300 Chestnut Street, Suite 200, Philadelphia, PA 19103, call (800) 810-4145 x5000, or email special.markets@perseusbooks.com.

Book Design by Timm Bryson

Library of Congress Cataloging-in-Publication Data
    Russell, Alec, 1966-
    Bring me my machine gun : the battle for the soul of South Africa from Mandela to Zuma / Alec Russell.—1st ed.
        p. cm.
    Includes bibliographical references and index.
    ISBN 978-1-58648-738-6 (hardcover)
    1. South Africa—Politics and government—1994-2. African National Congress. 3. Mandela, Nelson, 1918-4. Mbeki, Thabo. 5. Zuma, Jacob. I. Title.
DT1971.R87 2009
968.06'5—dc22
                                                                2008055404

First Edition

10 9 8 7 6 5 4 3 2 1